HORSE ESCAPE ARTIST!

And More True Stories of Animals Behaving Badly

By Ashlee Brown Blewett

NATIONAL GEOGRAPHIC

WASHINGTON, D.C.

Published by the National Geographic Society

John M. Fahey, *Chairman of the Board and Chief Executive Officer*
Declan Moore, *Executive Vice President; President, Publishing and Travel*
Melina Gerosa Bellows, *Publisher and Chief Creative Officer, Books, Kids, and Family*

Prepared by the Book Division

Hector Sierra, *Senior Vice President and General Manager*
Nancy Laties Feresten, *Senior Vice President, Kids Publishing and Media*
Jennifer Emmett, *Vice President, Editorial Director, Kids Books*
Eva Absher-Schantz, *Design Director, Kids Publishing and Media*
Jay Sumner, *Director of Photography, Kids Publishing*
R. Gary Colbert, *Production Director*
Jennifer A. Thornton, *Director of Managing Editorial*

Staff for This Book

Shelby Alinsky, *Project Editor*
Lisa Jewell, *Illustrations Editor*
Amanda Larsen, *Art Director*
Ruth Ann Thompson, *Designer*
Grace Hill, *Associate Managing Editor*
Michael O'Connor, *Production Editor*
Marfé Ferguson Delano, *Editor*
Lewis R. Bassford, *Production Manager*
Susan Borke, *Legal and Business Affairs*
Ariane Szu-Tu, *Editorial Assistant*
Callie Broaddus, *Design Production Assistant*
Margaret Leist, *Photo Assistant*

Production Services

Phillip L. Schlosser, *Senior Vice President*
Chris Brown, *Vice President, NG Book Manufacturing*
George Bounelis, *Senior Production Manager*
Nicole Elliott, *Director of Production*
Rachel Faulise, *Manager*
Robert L. Barr, *Manager*

For more information, please visit www.nationalgeographic.com, call 1-800-NGS LINE (647-5463), or write to the following address:

National Geographic Society, 1145 17th Street N.W., Washington, D.C. 20036-4688 U.S.A.

Visit us online at www.nationalgeographic.com/books

For librarians and teachers: www.ngchildrensbooks.org

National Geographic supports K–12 educators with ELA Common Core Resources. Visit natgeoed.org/commoncore for more information.

More for kids from National Geographic: kids.nationalgeographic.com

For information about special discounts for bulk purchases, please contact National Geographic Books Special Sales: ngspecsales@ngs.org

For rights or permissions inquiries, please contact National Geographic Books Subsidiary Rights: ngbookrights@ngs.org

Trade paperback
ISBN: 978-1-4263-1767-5
Reinforced library edition
ISBN: 978-1-4263-1768-2

Printed in China
14/RRDS/1

Table of CONTENTS

Mariska sticks her head out her stall-door window and tries to lift the door latch open.

MARISKA: HORSE ESCAPE ARTIST

Mariska wears colorful reindeer antlers to celebrate her first Christmas at Misty Meadows Farm.

Chapter 1

A FAIRY-TALE HORSE

It was a sunny morning in Midland, Michigan, U.S.A. A cool breeze blew through an open kitchen window at the Bonem home on Misty Meadows Farm. Mrs. Sandy Bonem was getting ready to cook breakfast.

Suddenly, a big black shadow loomed past the window. Wait! Make that *three* big black shadows. Mrs. Bonem glanced out the window, and her heart sank to her toes.

"HON!" she yelled across the house to her husband, Don Bonem. "The horses are out! They're in the backyard!"

Mrs. Bonem dashed to the back door. Slowly, she slid open the door and stepped onto the deck. "Trienke (sounds like TREN-kuh)," Mrs. Bonem called softly. She inched down the stairs. She stepped onto a thick bed of green grass and stopped. She didn't want to startle the herd.

The horses' ears twitched. They lifted their heads and turned toward the voice. Their bodies tensed. They could easily flee.

"Trienke, *come*," Mrs. Bonem said.

For a split second nothing happened. Then, all three horses lunged. They sprinted toward Mrs. Bonem like a pack of playful puppies. They kissed her cheeks with their big wet horse lips.

"Oh you guys!" she said. She stroked their foreheads and exhaled a deep sigh of relief. "How did you get out here?" She turned toward the barn. "Let's go," she said. All three horses followed her.

Minutes later, Mrs. Bonem reached the large sliding barn door. It looked like a clever horse had nudged it open. Mrs. Bonem turned and eyed the herd. Trienke is a ten-year-old mare, or female. She's the mother of the other two horses, Mariska (sounds like Muh-RIS-kah) and Wietse (sounds like WEET-sah).

Trienke is the boss mare, or leader, of

Did You Know?

There are about 400 types, or breeds, of horses.

the herd. But Mrs. Bonem knew that Trienke didn't always call the shots. Instead, Mrs. Bonem fingered Mariska as the guilty one. Mariska had a long record of making mischief.

The Misty Meadows horses are a breed known as Friesian (sounds like FREE-shun). Friesian horses come from Friesland (sounds like FREES-land)—a region of the Netherlands, a country in Europe. Friesians have all-black, shiny coats. And they're strong.

Long ago, Friesian horses carried knights into battle. "They look like a fairy-tale horse," Mrs. Bonem says. That's what first made her fall in love with the breed.

When Mr. and Mrs. Bonem decided to buy their first horse, it was a Friesian, of course. But first they built a barn. And instead of building just one horse stall in it, they built ten. With the extra room, other people could pay the Bonems to keep their horses at Misty Meadows, too.

A short while later, a family that lived down the street asked the Bonems to keep their two quarter horses at Misty Meadows. And the Bonems bought Trienke, their first Friesian.

Trienke was five years old when the Bonems got her in 2003. The next spring she gave birth to Mariska. Now the Bonems had four horses to look after.

As a baby, Mariska was allowed out of her stall to roam the barn during the day. The young horse followed Mrs. Bonem everywhere.

Born to Be Wild

Wild horses live in family groups called herds. Herd members form strong bonds, or ties. They nuzzle each other's faces and necks. Each herd member has a specific place, or rank, in the group. The same is true for pet horses. The horses higher up in rank protect those lower down the line. Horses like to be near other horses. This is true even if they're not related. Pet horses even treat humans like members of their herd.

Soon Mariska had Mrs. Bonem's heart wrapped around her tiny little hooves. Mariska's antics, or pranks, began when she was about six months old. Mrs. Bonem entered the horse's stall one morning. Mariska walked over. She nuzzled Mrs. Bonem's neck. Then she wrapped her teeth around the zipper tab on Mrs. Bonem's coat.

ZIP, ZIP! Mariska pulled the zipper up and down. Up and down. "You silly horse," Mrs. Bonem said.

Next, Mariska targeted hair ties. Whenever Mrs. Bonem bent down to clean her stall, Mariska lurked nearby. With one yank she would pull the fluffy red or blue hair tie off of Mrs. Bonem's ponytail. Then she'd try to eat it! *Chomp, chomp.*

Mrs. Bonem then had to pull the slimy lump of cloth out of Mariska's mouth. "*Errgh,* Mariska. Yuck!" She'd say.

Later that year, Mariska gave the Bonems a big scare. Snow was beginning to fall at the farm. To celebrate Mariska's first Christmas, Mrs. Bonem bought a pair of red-and-green reindeer antlers with small jingle bells attached to them.

Mrs. Bonem planned to take a picture of Mariska wearing the antlers. She headed to the barn with her camera. She laid the antlers on the windowsill and began brushing Mariska's coat. Mariska eyed the antlers. She inched toward the window. Then she snatched the antlers. *Ching, ching!*

"Mariska, NO!" Mrs. Bonem said.

She tugged on the antlers. Mariska let go. But one of the jingle bells was missing.

Mrs. Bonem pried open Mariska's mouth and felt around with her hand. *It's got to be in here somewhere,* she thought. GULP. Mariska swallowed the jingle bell. Mrs. Bonem quickly called the doctor. Could a tiny jingle bell hurt Mariska? Luckily, the answer was no. *Phew!*

Mariska's minor pranks continued for a few more years. She zipped and unzipped coats. She snatched lots of hair ties. She even learned to nudge open the grain bin and sneak extra meals. With each new trick Mariska learned, she got better at using her teeth. But as Mariska grew older, she got bored with zippers and hair ties. She was ready for a bigger challenge.

It looks like something has caught Mariska's eye. Watch out—she might be dreaming up her next prank!

Chapter 2

A PUZZLE SOLVED

When Mariska was three years old, Trienke gave birth to another foal, or baby horse. The Bonems named the little male Wietse. Not long afterward, Mariska had a foal of her own—a male named Arie.

Mariska played with Arie. She looked after him. For nearly a year, the foal even distracted Mariska from her silly games. Then a loving family from Florida adopted Arie. Soon after that, Mariska returned to making mischief.

One spring day in March 2009, Mrs. Bonem walked out to the barn. She threw some hay into each stall and flipped open the stall-door windows. As soon as Mrs. Bonem was out of sight, Mariska leaned out her window. She eyed the silver bolt that locked her door shut.

Mariska had seen Mrs. Bonem unlock this latch hundreds of times. Now, the horse grabbed the bolt with her teeth. She flipped it up and down. Finally, she slid the bolt over.

CLICK! The door opened. Mariska escaped into the small paddock (sounds

Did You Know?

Horses have the largest eyes of any land mammal.

like PAD-ock), or fenced-in area, outside her stall.

A short while later, Mrs. Bonem walked past. *That's strange,* she thought. *Did I forget to lock the door?* She led Mariska into her stall and slid the bolt into place. Mariska slid it back. CLICK! The door opened again.

"You clever horse!" Mrs. Bonem gasped.

The next day, Mr. Bonem attached a second bolt to the bottom of Mariska's door. *There's no way Mariska can reach this bolt,* he thought. Mariska tried another tactic. She unlocked the top bolt. Then she leaned hard against the door.

Mariska knew that if she pushed hard enough, things might break. She had learned this a few years ago, when she and the other Friesians wanted to eat the grass on the other side of their paddock. They craned their necks over the fence. They leaned hard against the wood, trying to reach the grass. Then, SNAP! The fence board broke.

Now one bolt stood between Mariska and the paddock. She leaned hard against the door. Finally, the bottom bolt snapped. Mariska stepped into the paddock. Then she unlocked Trienke and Wietse's stall doors. Now, all the Friesians were out.

Mr. and Mrs. Bonem's jaws dropped. They threw their hands in the air. Finally they decided to leave Mariska's outside stall door unlocked. It was better she escape to the paddock than break another door, they agreed.

Horse Sense

What do *you* do if faced with a problem? Probably you think about how to solve it. That's what humans do. Not horses, says horse behavior expert Dr. Cindy McCall. Horses learn through trial and error. Dr. McCall thinks Mariska probably first opened her stall door by accident. She was playing with the latch, and it flipped open. "But that doesn't mean horses aren't smart," Dr. McCall says. Horses have good memories. Once Mariska learned to open her door, doing it again was a breeze.

But Mariska had other plans. She shifted her attention to her inside stall door. Instead of leading outside into the paddock, this door led into the main aisle of the barn. That's where the Bonems kept the grain.

Mariska wrapped her teeth around the thin bar that locked this door in place. The bar was slippery. But Mariska kept trying. Finally, she lifted the bar toward the ceiling. CLICK! The door slid open.

Mariska made a beeline to the grain bin. She flipped open the lid. *Chomp, chomp.*

Now Mr. and Mrs. Bonem started to worry. Inside the barn, Mariska could make real trouble. She could cross the aisle and open the quarter horses' stall doors, too. But how could they stop her from escaping? They thought and thought.

Meanwhile, they tried to horse-proof the barn. First, they chained the grain bin under the counter. But Mariska broke the chain. Next, they poured the grain into an empty freezer chest in another room. Mariska quickly sniffed it out. For every move the Bonems made, Mariska had an answer.

That's enough! thought Mr. Bonem. He slung a heavy chain around the grain-room door and locked it with a padlock. *Take that, Mariska!*

But Mariska just moved on to another prank. She escaped her stall again. This time she nudged open the large sliding barn door that leads to the Bonems' backyard. That's when Mrs. Bonem found

Mariska, Trienke, and Wietse looming outside her kitchen window that sunny spring morning.

Finally, Mr. Bonem had another idea. He drilled a small hole into the bar that locks each stall door shut. He slipped a pin into the hole and pulled up on the bar. CLANK! The bar hit the pin and stopped. The door didn't budge. *There is no way Mariska can escape now,* he thought. *It's the perfect plan.*

Mr. Bonem was right. It was the perfect plan—as long as he and his wife remembered to slip the safety pins in place. But sometimes they forgot. Mariska made a game out of checking the bars in each stall door. CLANK. CLANK. If the Bonems forgot the pins, CLICK!

Mariska opened the door, and all the Friesians escaped.

Luckily, Mariska never bothered to free the quarter horses. Still, after a few backyard escapes by the Friesians, the Bonems buckled down. They checked and rechecked the pins. Soon, they opened the gates to the horses' grassy pastures.

The sweet grass distracted Mariska for a while. She seemed to forget about escaping. Weeks passed, and the Bonems forgot, too. Sometimes they forgot to pin the doors. Then one summer day, the unthinkable happened. Mariska gave the Bonems the scare of their lives.

Mariska's foal Siska stands next to her mother shortly after she is born. Will the foal be as adventurous as her escape artist mother?

The Friesians had grazed all the grass in their pasture by late summer. All that remained were nubs. Even the quarter horses' pasture next to theirs was looking bare. Soon, Mariska and the other Friesians began eyeing the thick yummy grass in the Bonems' backyard again. Only this time, Mariska decided the quarter horses should join in, too.

She sauntered over to the metal gate that linked the two pastures. She leaned her big, heavy body into it.

Soon, the gate started to budge. It was nearly there. If Mariska could just … She leaned harder. Harder. SNAP! The latch broke. The gate swung open.

Now Trienke, Wietse, and the two quarter horses followed Mariska through the paddock and into her stall. CLICK. She lifted the bar and slid the door open. The clever horse must have started checking again. And today was her lucky day. Someone had forgotten to set the safety pin.

Next, Mariska nudged open the large sliding barn door that leads outside.

Mariska's plan was probably the same

as before: escape to the backyard and eat as much grass as she could before getting caught. But the quarter horses had a different plan.

As soon as Mariska slid the barn door open, ZOOM! The quarter horses took off at a full gallop. The Friesians followed.

Meanwhile, a car had pulled into the driveway. A man and a woman got out of it. They looked up in time to see five large horses galloping straight toward them.

ZOOM! The couple jumped out of the way as the horses raced past.

Just then, Mr. Bonem looked out his office window. He saw five blurry streaks galloping full speed ahead toward the busy highway. *The quarter horses?* he thought. *How did they ...?* NOOOOOOO!

Natural-Born Runners

Wild horses are natural prey animals. This means that other animals hunt them. For this reason, horses stay alert. A horse's large eyes and keen ears are always looking and listening for danger. The faintest noise can make them RUN! Long legs and strong muscles give them speed. Hard hooves protect their feet as they pound the ground. And horses are the only mammals besides humans that produce a lot of sweat. Sweat cools a horse, allowing it to run fast over long distances.

By now, the Bonems didn't panic at the sight of Friesians in their backyard. Even though it was frustrating, they could always get the Friesians back into the barn. But the quarter horses had never escaped before. And the Bonems were responsible for them. What if they ran away? Or worse, what if they got hit by a car?

Mr. Bonem sprinted through the house and flung open the front door.

"Trienke!" he called. But by now the horses were out of range. They couldn't hear Mr. Bonem. So he lifted his pinky fingers to his lips and whistled as loud as he could. *Tsuweet!*

Trienke put on her brakes. Mariska and Wietse stopped, too. They looked back toward Mr. Bonem. The quarter horses kept going. Would the Friesians return?

Nope. They took off again toward the quarter horses.

"Stay here!" Mr. Bonem said to his friends. "Keep an eye on the horses!" He raced to the barn and grabbed a big gray bucket. He scooped it full of grain and rushed back outside.

Tsuweet! He whistled again.

This time, the Friesians froze. Mr. Bonem held the grain bucket high in the air. He shook it as loud as he could. The Friesians knew this sound. They knew this gray bucket. It was the one Mrs. Bonem shook at feeding time. Rattling inside were sweet morsels of grain. This time, Mariska, Trienke, and Wietse turned and headed back toward Mr. Bonem.

He led the Friesians to the barn and dropped the bucket on the floor. Then he grabbed two halters and another bucket of grain, and he dropped the hatch on the sliding barn door. He sprinted back to the front of the house. By now Mr. Bonem was panting hard. But he couldn't give up.

In the distance, the quarter horses had paused at the edge of the highway. Mr. Bonem slowed to a walk. He didn't want to scare them. Again, he lifted the grain bucket up high. SHAKE, SHAKE. RATTLE, RATTLE.

The quarter horses' eyes widened. They strained their necks and twitched their ears forward. *Can they see the bucket?* Mr. Bonem wondered. It seemed like it. They stood as still as deer in the woods. Yes, Mr. Bonem had their attention! He was sure of it. Slowly, he crept toward them. He was thirty feet away. Twenty. Ten.

The horses' nostrils flared. They inched toward Mr. Bonem. Carefully, he placed a rope over the first horse's neck. Then the next one. Finally he slipped on their halters. The quarter horses were safe at last.

Phew, Mr. Bonem thought. *That was a close call. Too close.*

Ever since that scary day, the Bonems have been extra cautious. They double-check the pins when they leave a stall. And they keep a lookout for weak gate latches and loose boards.

Now it's more important than ever. Mariska recently gave birth to her second foal—a female named Siska. And Siska has already proven to be a brave little explorer.

At only six months old, the foal slips out any open door she sees, with or without her mama. She has even escaped the stall they share with no help from Mariska. How? By leaping out the open stall-door window!

"It looks like Siska is for sure going to take after her mama," Mrs. Bonem says. "Only apparently she thinks she is a jumper!"

Did You Know?

When a horse flicks one ear forward and the other ear back, it is alert. When it pins both ears back, it usually means it is angry.

Milkshake looks ready to party in her purple cowboy hat, but first she stops to pose for the camera. Say "cheese"!

MILKSHAKE:
THE CHARGING COW

Milkshake is ready to be led on a walk around the Grace Foundation.

Chapter 1

No Ordinary COW

The sound of heavy hooves hitting cement echoed through a large ranch in El Dorado Hills, California, U.S.A. CLOP. CLOP. CLOP. Milkshake the cow moseyed up the sidewalk. She stopped outside an open door and looked up. A wooden sign read "Cowgirls." Milkshake entered.

Outside the sun shone bright. But inside the room was dim.

It took the cow's eyes time to adjust. When they did, Milkshake found herself standing in front of a sink. She was in the ranch's bathroom. She glanced up at a large mirror on the wall. Her eyes widened. *Humph!* She blew a puff of air through her nose.

Staring back at Milkshake was another cow. It looked just like her. *Yikes!*

Milkshake panicked. She shuffled her burly body backward. CLATTER, BANG, BOOM! A trash can crashed to the floor. Dust flew. Milkshake bolted out the bathroom door like a high-speed bullet train.

It was the first time the cow had seen her reflection. But what in the world was a cow doing in a bathroom?

Milkshake is no ordinary cow. And the ranch where Milkshake lives is no ordinary ranch. It's home to the Grace Foundation. Grace is a group that rescues animals whose owners don't take care of them.

Grace's goal is to make each animal better. They bring in veterinarians (sounds like vet-er-ih-NARE-ee-ens) to treat the animals that are hurt or sick.

There are many horses at Grace, along with some cows, sheep, llamas, chickens, and other animals. As soon as an animal is healthy, Grace usually looks for a loving family to adopt it. But a few of the rescued animals get to stay at Grace for good.

The animals that stay have important jobs. They are called animal educators. They help teach children who visit the ranch about farm animals. Today Milkshake is one of the animal educators. But her first few months at Grace were rocky.

Milkshake arrived at the ranch in 2008. She was small and shy. She was about two years old. Her previous owner had kept her locked in a filthy pen. The pen was so small it stunted, or slowed down, Milkshake's growth.

Milkshake is a Hereford (sounds like HER-furd) cow. Herefords are a large breed of cattle. A two-year-old normally weighs about 1,000 pounds (450 kg). But Milkshake weighed only half that!

Besides locking Milkshake in a tiny pen, Milkshake's owner didn't talk to her. She didn't pet her. And she separated Milkshake from other animals.

Cow Chow

Most cows eat grass. But grass is not an easy food to digest. This makes eating an all-day task. First, good bacteria in the cow's stomach help break down the grass. Then the cow spits up partly digested food called cud. It chews the cud for about eight hours. Then—GULP!—the cow swallows the cud. It travels back through the cow's four-part stomach where more bacteria help the cow digest the food for good. There's only one problem. Smelly bacteria give the cow stinky breath. *Pee-yew!*

At Grace, things were different. Milkshake lived in a large, grassy pasture.

Several horses, goats, and chickens lived nearby. But Milkshake didn't roam the pasture or eat grass like a normal cow. She had never learned how. Instead, Milkshake stood there. Her head drooped toward the ground. "She looked tiny and sad," says Beth DeCaprio.

Beth is the Grace Foundation's director. She fell in love with Milkshake the first time she saw her. She wanted to help the cow make new friends. But every time she walked out to greet Milkshake, the cow backed away.

How can I get this cow to trust me? Beth wondered. Finally, she just plopped down on the grass in Milkshake's pasture.

Day after day, she sat there. Then after several days, Milkshake approached Beth.

Beth slowly put out her hand. She reached her arm up and petted Milkshake's head. Then, being careful not to startle the cow, she rose to her feet. She rubbed the cow's back and scratched her neck. Milkshake leaned hard into Beth's hand. To the cow it probably felt like when a friend scratches an itch in the middle of your back that you can't reach. *Ahhhhh.*

Soon, Milkshake held her head high. She roamed her pasture. And when Beth's car rolled into the gravel parking lot, Milkshake called out to her. *Mooo! Mooo!*

One day Beth slipped a halter and rope, called a lead, over Milkshake's head. A lead is like a leash for farm animals. Then the two friends walked out of the pasture. It was time for Milkshake to explore the ranch.

On her walks with Beth, Milkshake met other people who rubbed her back and scratched her neck. She would sniff their hands. Then she licked their arms with her long, slimy tongue. It was the cow's way of saying, "I like you!"

Soon Milkshake let children who visited the ranch pet her and talk to her. The patient cow would stand still for hours. And when the ranch hosted birthday parties, Beth strapped a pointed hat on Milkshake's head. Then everyone sang "Happy Birthday."

Milkshake loved getting so much attention. She became more confident. Eventually, Beth let Milkshake off her lead. Now, Milkshake had the run of the ranch.

Milkshake followed Beth everywhere. She climbed up the steps and into the ranch office. She stood by the picnic tables at lunch. She even followed Beth into the bathroom. That's where the cow saw her reflection in the mirror for the first time. Beth laughs, "Every time she went in there, it scared her!"

By the end of her first summer at Grace, Milkshake's life had completely changed. She had grown to 900 pounds (410 kg). And she had made lots of new friends. Everyone agreed: The cow didn't have a naughty bone in her body. Or did she?

A crouching Milkshake lowers her head and narrows her eyes. She looks ready to charge!

Chapter 2

A Cow With a Grudge

During that fall, the Grace Foundation rescued 60 animals in one day. Workers quickly built fences on every open corner of the ranch to hold the new animals. One new pasture sat in Lisa Dowling's front yard.

Lisa is the ranch manager at Grace. She lives there in a small house near the main office building. Beth decided to move

Milkshake into the new pasture in Lisa's yard. Now, Milkshake would be near Beth even when she was in her pasture.

Every morning, Lisa woke before the sun rose. She poured coffee in a to-go cup and walked outside to check on the animals. Usually a big, shaggy, white dog named Sam greeted Lisa at her back door. Sam was the ranch's patrol dog. He walked with Lisa on her morning rounds.

But one morning Sam didn't show. Lisa peered out her back window. The dog was nowhere in sight. *That's strange,* she thought. *Where could he be?* She walked through the house and out the front door into Milkshake's pasture.

It was still dark, but Lisa could see that the dog lay in a heap on the ground.

Milkshake stood over him. "Sam!" Lisa called. The dog whimpered, but he didn't move. Lisa ran to the dog's side. She grabbed his back end and tried to lift him. The dog yelped in pain.

Milkshake hovered over them. Afraid the cow might step on the dog, Lisa yelled at Milkshake to move. But the cow stood firm. Lisa's heart thumped against her chest. Her panic turned to fear.

"Milkshake, move!" Lisa yelled again. She tried to push the cow away, but it was no use. Milkshake wouldn't budge.

Now Lisa was scared for the dog's life. So she did the only thing she could think of. She grabbed a saddle strap that hung over the fence. She swatted Milkshake with it. But the stubborn cow just stared at her.

Anger and fear bubbled up inside Lisa. Just then Beth's car pulled into the parking lot. She hopped out of the car and ran to the pasture. She was able to lure Milkshake away from the dog.

Then Beth and Lisa scooped Sam off the ground. They loaded him into the car and drove to the veterinarian. Luckily, the doctor said Sam would be okay. He guessed another animal had kicked the dog. A shot of medicine eased Sam's pain. Two hours later the dog could walk.

Phew! Lisa and Beth thought.

Did Milkshake accidentally kick or step on Sam? Lisa wondered. *Or was she trying to protect the dog by standing guard over him?* There was no way to know. But it didn't really matter. Lisa felt bad for swatting Milkshake. But she was glad Sam was okay. Lisa quickly forgot about the morning's events.

Milkshake, however, did not forget.

A week later, Lisa and Beth were walking by the pond when Milkshake came up. The cow looked at Lisa. Her eyes narrowed. Her nostrils flared. She dropped her big, heavy head. Then she rammed it into Lisa's stomach! Lisa stumbled backward.

Beth quickly stepped in, and Milkshake walked away. Lisa glanced at Beth, who laughed nervously. "She's just playing with you," Beth said. But Lisa wasn't so sure that Milkshake was just playing.

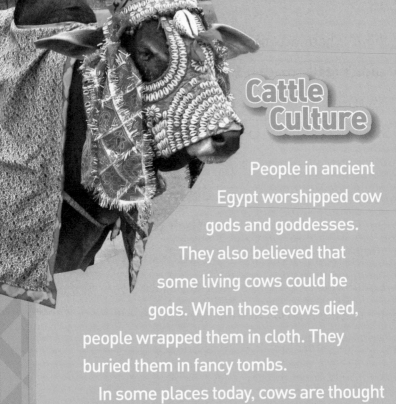

Cattle Culture

People in ancient Egypt worshipped cow gods and goddesses. They also believed that some living cows could be gods. When those cows died, people wrapped them in cloth. They buried them in fancy tombs.

In some places today, cows are thought to be holy, or sacred (sounds like SAY-krid). They are often allowed to roam free. In Delhi, India, about 40,000 cows roam the streets. Some people even feed the animals a piece of bread or fruit for good luck!

A couple of days later, Milkshake approached Lisa in the parking lot. Again, Milkshake's eyes narrowed. Her nostrils flared and she dropped her head. *Uh-oh*, Lisa thought. Then, BAM!

When Milkshake's head hit Lisa's stomach, Lisa slid backward across the gravel. This time the message was clear. Milkshake did NOT like Lisa anymore.

"I never knew a cow could hold a grudge," Lisa says. She tried to apologize to Milkshake for swatting her. But every time Lisa approached Milkshake, the cow charged. Even in large crowds, Milkshake managed to single Lisa out.

"It was like she had radar or something," Lisa says. So she decided to stay out of the cow's way. If Milkshake came around, Lisa either climbed onto a picnic table or quietly walked away. Even her own front yard was off-limits.

Lisa did her best to stay out of Milkshake's sight. But she was not out of the cow's mind. One day Milkshake turned her attention to Lisa's house.

Lisa was sitting on the couch in her front room. She heard a familiar sound. CLOP. CLOP. CLOP. She peered out the window. Sure enough, there was Milkshake. The cow stood at the top of the porch, staring through the window.

Then Milkshake turned toward the wooden porch railing. She leaned into it with her bulky frame. She kicked it with her hard hooves. And she beat it with her large, heavy head. After a while, SNAP!

One of the posts broke. Milkshake took two steps over and started on the next one.

Lisa couldn't believe her eyes. It was like Milkshake had two personalities. And Lisa only saw the angry one. "Maybe we should move Milkshake to another pasture," Lisa said to Beth. But the ranch was totally full. There was nowhere else to put the crabby cow.

Over the next few months, Milkshake slowly demolished Lisa's porch. She kicked posts out of the porch railing. She tore the hand railing off the steps. And she licked a corner of the house over and over. Finally, a chunk of it fell off.

But this was only the beginning. "After that," Lisa says, "Milkshake got really destructive."

No matter how much trouble Milkshake causes, her best friend Beth stands by her side.

Chapter 3

Water, Water, EVERYWHERE!

As Milkshake's relationship with Lisa got worse, her friendship with Beth grew stronger. It was rare to see Beth without the cow.

"If the door to the classroom was open, Milkshake was in there," Beth says. And the cow refused to wait her turn. She pushed past other people. Then she squeezed through the door.

By now, Milkshake was like an army tank. If something sat in her path, she ran right through it. Tables and chairs scraped across the floor. Crayons and papers flew through the air. And every now and then, Milkshake left behind a special surprise. A smelly cow pie!

Over time, Milkshake's manners went from bad to worse. The greedy cow couldn't keep out of the grain barrel. She would knock the lid off and help herself to the food.

One day Beth saw Milkshake stumbling around outside. The grain barrel was stuck on her head! The cow shook her massive head from side to side. But it was no use. Finally Beth had to pull the barrel off.

As Milkshake grew bigger, she got

bolder. She knocked over hay bales in the barn. She dumped the dogs' water buckets and splashed in the puddles. And when it was time to take Milkshake to the vet, the stubborn cow refused to walk up the ramp into the truck trailer.

Every time it was the same. Beth would press on Milkshake's backside. This was the signal for her to move forward. But Milkshake stood strong.

"Come on, Milkshake," Beth would say, laughing. "Let's go." Then two people would try pushing the cow from behind. But if a full-grown cow doesn't want to move, she won't. Milkshake dug in her hooves. She stayed planted on the ground.

By now it was clear to everyone at Grace: Milkshake ruled the ranch.

Then one evening, Beth forgot to put Milkshake back in her pasture before she left for home. That was a HUGE mistake.

Errn! Errn! Errn! Lisa's alarm clock sounded early the next morning. She climbed out of bed and walked to the bathroom. She squeezed a lump of toothpaste onto her toothbrush. But when she twisted the faucet handle, nothing came out. The faucet was bone-dry.

Milkshake, Lisa thought to herself. She had noticed that Beth had left Milkshake out the night before. But she sure wasn't going to put the charging cow away. She had learned better than to get too close to Milkshake.

Lisa walked back to her bedroom and glanced out the window. *Oh no.*

Cow Power

Thirty thousand dairy cows live at Fair Oaks Farms in Indiana, U.S.A. But the cows there don't just produce milk. They help run the farm. How? With their poop! Farmworkers collect about 5 million pounds (2.2 million kg) of manure from the Fair Oaks barns every day. Then they run the poop through special machines. The machines turn the poop into clean energy and natural gas. The energy powers the farm. And the natural gas fuels the farm's 42 delivery trucks. Now that's cow power.

Milkshake had been on a path of destruction. Everywhere Lisa looked, water gushed out of the ground like a geyser (sounds like GUY-zer). Milkshake had broken three pipes.

Lisa sighed. She pulled on her clothes and ran out the door. She turned off the water supply at each pipe. Then she walked to the barn. She took a deep breath. *First things first,* she said to herself. *Feed the animals, then fix the pipes.*

After that, Beth was careful to keep Milkshake penned in her pasture. The unpredictable cow could come out only to teach the children. Of course, this did not go over well with Milkshake. As soon as Beth's car pulled into the driveway, the cow ran to her gate. *Mooo! Mooo!* she called to Beth. Beth tried to ignore her. But even inside the office, Beth could hear Milkshake. *Moooo! Moooooo!* she bawled.

This broke Beth's heart. Every so often she gave in. "I'll just let her out for a little while," she'd say. But every time, Milkshake returned to her old tricks. She even broke several more pipes.

And if the cow saw Lisa, she charged. "Please keep Milkshake in her pasture," Lisa begged Beth. By now Lisa had given up hope that she and Milkshake would ever be friends. Then, one afternoon, she found new hope.

Did You Know?

Cows eat about 40 pounds (18 kg) of food each day and drink around 30 gallons (110 L) of water.

Lisa was walking out her back door. She looked up to see Beth and Milkshake in her yard. "Oh good grief," Lisa said. But before she could escape, Beth caught her attention.

"Come here, please," Beth said. "Just pet Milkshake. I won't let her hurt you."

Normally, Lisa would have said, "No, thanks." But Beth had Milkshake on a lead. And something about the cow seemed different today. Her eyes looked soft. Her breath was slow. And she held her head high. Lisa walked over. She took a deep breath and reached out her hand. This time, Milkshake stood still.

Lisa smiled. She couldn't believe it. She rubbed Milkshake's back and scratched her neck. *Hmm*, Lisa thought. *Maybe Milkshake finally realizes that I'm not so bad after all.*

Was this the beginning of a new friendship? Only time will tell.

Milkshake still lives at the Grace Foundation. She continues to teach children about cattle. And she's still a big hit at birthday parties. Now Milkshake is even part of a therapy program. Children who don't like to talk practice reading books to Milkshake. Milkshake is a good listener. But with Lisa things are still a little shaky.

"It's hot and cold with Milkshake now," Lisa says. Milkshake sometimes still tries to charge Lisa. But Lisa is hopeful. She shared a sweet moment with the cow. "It happened, and that's what I'm hanging on to," she says. "Who knows? It could happen again!"

Pony the goat takes time out from making mischief to give three barnyard friends a piggy-back ride.

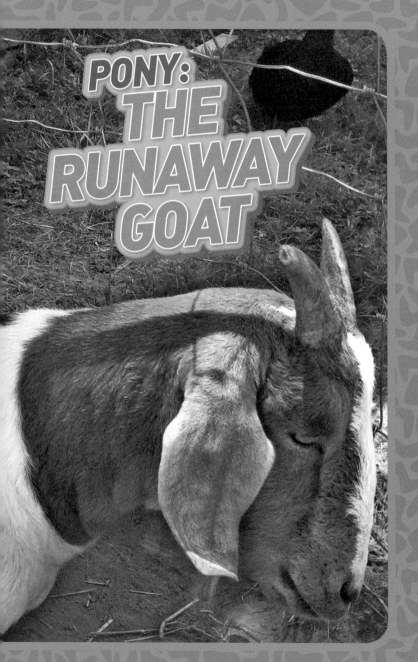

PONY: THE RUNAWAY GOAT

Pony keeps a close eye on the man building a fence. Pony doesn't care much for fences.

Chapter 1

GOATS on the Loose!

CLINK-*CLANK*. CLINK-*CLANK*. It was June 2009, in Riverdale, Georgia, U.S.A. Chad Artimovich (sounds like ART-ih-MO-vich) was pounding metal fence posts into the ground. *I'll get them this time,* he muttered to himself. Chad was building a large catch pen behind an apartment building. His target? Two runaway goats. The pair had been making mischief there for months. No one had been able to catch them.

No one knew where the goats had come from. But they likely escaped from a nearby farm. The buck, or male goat, was all black with a long beard. The doe, or female goat, was white with a rusty-red face and a big round belly. A yellow tag dangled from each of the goats' ears. Farmers use this kind of tag to keep track of their animals. But no one claimed the goats.

Now the goats were bandits. Outlaws. And they had decided to make the woods behind the Chase Ridge Apartments in Riverdale their home.

Did You Know?

Nearly three million goats live in the United States today.

Goats are hardy animals. This means they can adapt to many habitats, because they eat foods that most other animals would not eat. Goats feast on weeds, leaves, brush, twigs, and tree bark. There was plenty of food behind the Chase Ridge Apartments. But the goats were not exactly friendly to their new neighbors.

One resident came face-to-face with the male goat. "When I was looking at him, he was looking at me," he said. "And he was coming charging at me. And I just ran right across the street." As the weeks passed, the goats became more daring.

Another neighbor opened his door to find the male goat staring up at him. The man quickly slammed the door shut. But the bold goats did not give up. Later the female broke into another apartment. The goat knocked the door open. She ran inside and tore through the rooms. Then she left—leaving a mess behind her.

Word about the gutsy goats spread fast. One day a TV news crew showed up at the apartment to film them. The goats became famous!

But what had caused the goats to be so bold? Why would they break into an apartment? It's possible they were thirsty. The woods offered plenty of food but little fresh water for the goats to drink. It was especially important for the female to find water, because she was pregnant! But that didn't win her much sympathy. Their new neighbors were fed up with the goats' bad behavior. They began to complain.

The local animal control team tried nabbing the goats first. They chased the pair with a catch pole. A catch pole is a long pole with a loop on the end. If they could slip the loop over the goats' heads, they could catch them. But every time the team got near enough to use the pole, the goats sprinted deeper into the woods. It was time to call in the experts.

The Chase Ridge Apartments manager phoned a company called Atlanta Wildlife Solutions. Chad Artimovich was the owner. Could *he* help catch the goats? It would be a tough job. But Chad had rescued many tricky animals before. "Yes," he said. He would find a way to round up the sneaky goats.

Chad drove his truck to the apartment

building. The goats had wandered into a grassy area next to the building. He and two crew members surrounded the pair. The goats tensed. Their tails curled over their backs. And their ears pricked forward. *Choo!* One of the goats sniffed. The men advanced. The goats ran for it, but everywhere they turned a large man stood waiting to catch them.

Working together, the men herded the goats toward a corner of the building. Chad wrapped his arms around the female. He had caught her! But not for long. The wriggly goat slipped through his fingers and darted back into the woods. Chad grumbled. Then he came up with a new plan. He would build a large pen with a gate and trap the goats inside.

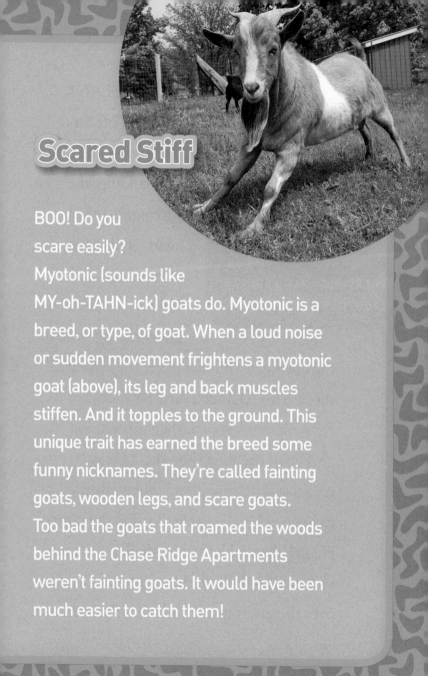

Scared Stiff

BOO! Do you scare easily? Myotonic (sounds like MY-oh-TAHN-ick) goats do. Myotonic is a breed, or type, of goat. When a loud noise or sudden movement frightens a myotonic goat (above), its leg and back muscles stiffen. And it topples to the ground. This unique trait has earned the breed some funny nicknames. They're called fainting goats, wooden legs, and scare goats.

Too bad the goats that roamed the woods behind the Chase Ridge Apartments weren't fainting goats. It would have been much easier to catch them!

CLINK-*CLANK*. CLINK-*CLANK*.

"All done," Chad said, dusting off his hands. The next time the goats came near the building, the men surrounded them again. This time they chased the goats toward the pen. The goats ran right up to the open gate. But suddenly they stopped short. They changed direction. Instead of running into the pen, they ran around it!

Darn! the men thought. "Okay," Chad said. "New plan." He walked over to his truck and reached inside the door. He grabbed a big bag of shelled corn and returned to the pen. He scattered the corn over the grass inside the pen. Then the

Did You Know?

Goats make a high-pitched noise that sounds like a sneeze when they sense danger.

men climbed into the truck and drove off. This time, *they* would be the tricky ones.

Later that night, Chad returned to the apartment building. By now it was dark. The neighbors were fast asleep indoors. The yard was quiet. Chad crept around the side of the building, careful not to make a sound. The goats were huddled together inside the pen. They were chomping on the corn. The trap had worked! Chad inched closer to the fence. At the back of the pen, he snapped the gate shut. The goats never saw it coming.

Now, one at a time, Chad walked the hoofed bandits to the truck. He lifted them into the covered back end and closed the hatch tight. It was time for the long drive to the goats' new home.

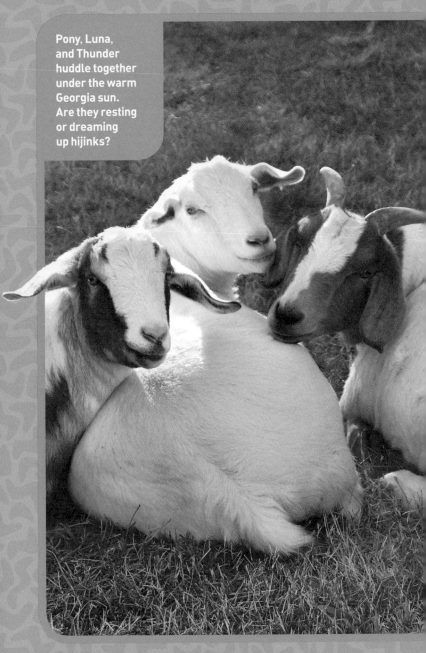

Pony, Luna, and Thunder huddle together under the warm Georgia sun. Are they resting or dreaming up hijinks?

Chapter 2

THREE'S A CROWD

Chad pulled the truck up to a pale yellow house in the sprawling countryside in Chattahoochee (sounds like CHAT-uh-HOO-chee) Hills, Georgia, U.S.A. He parked next to an open gate behind the house. Then he hopped out of the truck and flung open the back.

The goats rose to their feet and leaped onto the grass. They sprinted past a woman and three children, who were standing on the lawn in their pajamas. Then they disappeared into a cluster of trees at the far side of the yard.

Tom and Susan Tillander and their three children had moved into the pale yellow house a few months earlier. Before the move, they had lived in a crowded city suburb. The houses there sat close together.

The Tillander children—Molly, Jacob, and Alec—barely had room to play outside. Now they had a large, fenced-in backyard. An even bigger field lay behind the house. The children had space to play, and the family had plenty of land to raise animals, too.

Did You Know?

People around the world drink more milk from goats than from cows.

Mr. Tillander built a chicken coop behind the house. Mrs. Tillander stocked it full of chickens. And the family's two rescue dogs, Shiloh and Delilah, ran loose in the backyard. Mr. and Mrs. Tillander had also talked about getting goats. They wanted them. The problem was Mr. Tillander had to go away for work training. He had no time to build a fence around the field before he left. There was nowhere to put goats. The family would have to wait to get more animals until Mr. Tillander finished his training.

Only Mrs. Tillander couldn't wait. She saw the news story about the runaway goats. The goats needed a home. *We still have a fenced-in backyard,* she thought. So Mrs. Tillander called Atlanta Wildlife

Solutions. She offered to care for the goats. "If you can catch them," she said. Two days later, Chad delivered the goats to her backyard.

Each morning, Susan and Molly carried buckets of fresh water to the edge of the trees. But the goats refused to come out of the woods. To the goats, the woods probably felt safe. But soon after the goats arrived at their new home, the male goat fell ill. He had likely picked up a disease from living in the wild for so long. Sadly, he died. Now, with no mate to keep her company, the female came out of hiding.

Mrs. Tillander and Molly sat as still as statues on the porch. They smiled as the goat walked toward them. "What should we name her?" Mrs. Tillander whispered.

Goats Go Global

Long ago wild goats roamed across rugged mountains in the Middle East, Europe, and Asia. They were first tamed about 10,000 years ago. People living in what is now Iran began keeping them. Early farmers drank goat milk. They ate goat meat. And they made clothes from the goats' fur. Later, European settlers brought goats with them to the Americas. No goats had lived there before. They even set goats loose on islands along the way. Today more than 800 million goats live on the planet.

Just then the goat opened her mouth and let out a sound. *Maaa!* she cried. It sounded like a horse neighing. "Let's name her Pony!" Molly said. And they did.

Pony waddled right up to Mrs. Tillander and Molly, as if she'd never been afraid of them. The pregnant goat even let them pet her. "After that, she was with us every day," Mrs. Tillander says. Once Pony decided to trust the family, she planted herself at the back door and made herself at home.

She nibbled on Mrs. Tillander's freshly planted rose bushes. She chased Shiloh and Delilah around the backyard. And whenever the Tillanders walked outside, Pony ran over to greet them. She rubbed her big body against their legs. When they plopped down next to the goat, Pony laid her head in their laps like a pet dog. "We just sat with her, and petted her, and brushed her fur," Molly says.

Pony loved the attention. "Soon she wanted us with her all the time," Mrs. Tillander says. Wild goats are rarely alone. They live in family groups called herds. If no one was around to play with Pony, she would call for her new companions. *Maaa, maaa!* she'd cry.

The goat would even stand on her hind legs and peer through the back-door window. She'd slink along the back of the house, listening for voices. Goats have excellent hearing. If Pony heard the smallest noise, she would neigh. "It was like a child going, *'Mom! Mom!'*" Mrs. Tillander says.

Calling is how goats locate other herd members. By now it was clear to the Tillanders. They hadn't adopted Pony. She had adopted them.

About a month later, Pony started acting strangely. She walked around the yard and pawed at the ground. That night, Mrs. Tillander heard a muffled cry outside the window. *Ma, ma. Ma, ma.* Only it wasn't Pony. Mrs. Tillander knew what that sound meant.

"Pony had her kids!" she shouted. "Pony had her kids!" Mrs. Tillander and the children ran outside. There, under the porch, Pony lay on the ground. Curled up next to her were two tiny kids, or baby goats. One was pure white. The other looked just like Pony. The Tillanders

Female goats
give birth to
one to five kids.

named the kids Luna
and Thunder.

Luna and Thunder were bundles of
energy. They hopped across the yard as if
their legs were made of springs. When they
grew bigger, the playful pair climbed on
top of the picnic table. They bumped
heads. And they shoved each other to
see who could stay on top.

The Tillanders enjoyed watching the
kids play. But as Luna and Thunder
grew, the backyard began to shrink.
Every time the family stepped outside,
three rowdy goats mobbed them. If the
Tillanders sat down on the lawn, all three
goats clambered into their laps. The big
backyard, it seemed, had become a little
too crowded.

Luna and Thunder share a quiet moment. Most of the time, the two young goats are a handful!

Chapter 3

GATE-Crashers!

That August, Mr. Tillander returned home to Georgia. He was not surprised to see the goats. Mrs. Tillander had told him about them over the phone. But he was not pleased about them being in the backyard. Now he had a one-week break from his work training. He set to work building the goats a new enclosure in the field behind the house.

Mr. Tillander built a shelter for the goats to sleep in. And he dragged the picnic table into the pasture for Luna and Thunder to climb on. Now the goats would have plenty of space to play. And his family could walk outside without getting mobbed.

Over the next couple of weeks, Mrs. Tillander even bought a few turkeys and some ducks. Now the pasture was full of barnyard animals.

The goats seemed to enjoy their new home. Luna and Thunder battled on top of the picnic table. They scaled the woodpile next to their shelter.

Goats are master climbers. Two flexible toes on each hoof help them stay balanced on slippery surfaces. If Jacob or Alec left the tractor parked in the pasture, the goats climbed on top of it, too. Then one day, the goats set their sights on something else—something on the other side of the fence.

Ruff! Ruff! Shiloh and Delilah barked wildly. Molly ran to the window and peeked outside. The goats were next to the house nibbling Mrs. Tillander's rose bushes! Molly glanced at the pasture. The gate was shut tight.

How did those crazy goats get out? she wondered. Molly led the goats back to the pasture. But a couple of days later the sneaky goats escaped again!

> **Did You Know?**
>
> **Old Christmas trees and ripe pumpkins make tasty holiday treats for goats.**

Goats in Mythology

Ancient Greek and Roman people honored goats. The Greek god of nature—Pan—was half goat. He had a human body with the legs, horns, and ears of a goat. Pan ruled over goatlike spirits called satyrs (sounds like SAY-ters). He protected shepherds and their animals, too. In ancient Rome, the god Faunus (sounds like FAWN-us) was part goat. Faunus, shown above, also protected shepherds. And he roamed the woods with goatlike spirits called fauns. The Romans believed that the sounds of the forest were Faunus speaking.

It happened while Mr. Tillander was away at work and Mrs. Tillander was out running errands. Molly was in charge at home. She was outside with the dogs. Suddenly they heard a faint *clunk-clunk*. The dogs' ears perked up. *Ruff! Ruff!* They ran to the other side of the house. *Not again*, Molly thought.

She sprinted to catch up with the dogs. At the edge of the driveway she jolted to a stop. At first she couldn't believe her eyes. Pony and Thunder were standing on the roof of her father's car!

"Pony! Thunder! Get down!" Molly shouted at them.

But the goats didn't listen. Instead, they hopped from the roof of the car down to the hood. Then they sprinted up the windshield and onto the roof again. Luna was on the ground, running circles around the car. *Maaa! Maaa!* she cried.

Molly shouted at the goats again. Meanwhile, the racket attracted an audience.

Shiloh and Delilah barked wildly. The turkeys waddled over to the fence.

Gobble, gobble! they cried. The ducks and the chickens came to see the show, too. *Quack, quack, cluck, cluck.* It looked like a circus had landed in the Tillanders' driveway.

Thunder reared up on her hind legs. She smashed her front hooves down onto the roof of Mr. Tillander's car. Now Molly began to panic.

"Thunder!" she yelled. "Get down

now!" This time the goat listened. She jumped onto the ground.

"Phew," Molly sighed. But before she could grab the naughty goat, Thunder leaped onto the car again!

Just then Mrs. Tillander's car pulled into the driveway. Pony and Thunder's bodies tensed. They locked eyes with Mrs. Tillander. Before she even stepped out of her car, Pony and Thunder jumped to the ground. Then all three goats sprinted toward the pasture.

The trio skidded to a halt at the pasture gate. One by one, they squeezed through a small gap where the gate met the fence post. The gap was only a few inches wide. Still the goats managed to wriggle their fat bodies through!

Mrs. Tillander and Molly's mouths fell open. Were they dreaming? Nope. It turns out goats have a barnyard reputation for being difficult to fence in. But usually there is a reason why they break out. If a goat is hungry or bored, for example, it will find a way to escape.

But the Tillanders' goats had plenty of food to eat. And they had plenty of stuff to climb on. So why leave the pasture? "It could be that they just missed us," Mrs. Tillander says. "Or maybe it was payback for moving them away from the house."

But there was no turning back now. The damage had been done. The goats' hooves left dents the size of basketballs in the roof of Mr. Tillander's car.

Mrs. Tillander and Molly patched the

gap in the fence. They stacked cement blocks in front of the gate. They secured them with wire. Now no one—not even the Tillanders—could get through.

A few weeks later, Mr. Tillander returned home again. He looked at his goat-damaged car and shook his head. Then he examined every inch of the fence for gaps and loose panels. "All clear," he finally said.

But Mr. Tillander knows that goats are persistent. "If they want to get out, they'll find a way," he says.

And he was right. The clever goats did manage to escape a few more times. They even hopped on top of Mr. Tillander's car again. Luckily, though, he was able to get them off before they did any real damage.

It has been a couple of years now since the goats' car party. Over time, Pony, Thunder, and Luna have calmed down. But to Mrs. Tillander, things may be a little too quiet. She would like to see baby goats romping around the backyard again. But Mr. Tillander, well, he's not so sure that's a good idea.

THE END

DON'T MISS!

NATIONAL GEOGRAPHIC KiDS **CHAPTERS**

THE WHALE WHO WON HEARTS!

And More True Stories of Adventures With Animals

By Brian Skerry
with Kathleen Weidner Zoehfeld

**Turn the page
for a sneak preview . . .**

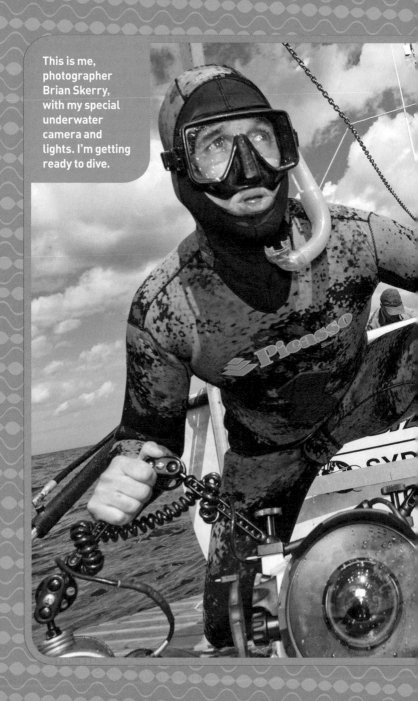

This is me, photographer Brian Skerry, with my special underwater camera and lights. I'm getting ready to dive.

Chapter 1

A SHOT in the DARK

It was a warm night in May. I was walking along a beach in Trinidad (sounds like TRIH-nuh-dad), an island in the Caribbean (sounds like CARE-uh-BEE-un) Sea. It was almost midnight. The ocean waves rumbled and crashed onto the sand. Behind the beach, palm trees swayed in the damp breeze.

Suddenly, a few yards down, I spotted dark shapes on the sand.

They looked like huge rocks. But they were leatherback sea turtles! They were here to do something sea turtles have been doing for more than 100 million years. And I was hoping to shoot them. With my camera, that is!

My name is Brian Skerry. I'm an underwater wildlife photographer. It's my job to take pictures of animals that live in the sea.

I fell in love with the sea when I was a child. I grew up in a small town in Massachusetts. We lived about an hour's drive from the ocean. I was always asking my parents to take me there.

When I wasn't at the beach, I was

reading books or watching TV shows about ocean life. I really admired the sea turtles. It was fun to imagine gliding with them through miles of deep, blue water.

When I was 15, I tried scuba diving. It was in my family's swimming pool. I was sitting in the shallow end. I had the scuba tank on my back. Hoses attached to the tank would bring air to my mouthpiece. I'll never forget putting that mouthpiece in and taking my first breath underwater. All I could think was, "Wow! I have discovered a whole new world!"

As I grew up, I practiced diving. I studied photography in college. I began taking underwater photos. Finally, I landed my dream job. I was hired to take photos for *National Geographic* magazine.

And that's what brought me to Trinidad. I was there to photograph sea turtles for National Geographic.

Sea turtles are reptiles. Like all reptiles, they breathe air. But unlike most reptiles, sea turtles don't live on land. They spend nearly their entire lives in the ocean. That's why they're called marine reptiles.

One hundred million years ago, dinosaurs ruled the land. At that time, many types of marine reptiles lived in the oceans. Giant, long-necked plesiosaurs (sounds like PLEEZ-ee-oh-soars) and sharp-toothed ichthyosaurs (sounds like ICK-thee-oh-soars) swam the seas. Earth's first sea turtles swam with them.

Dinosaurs died out 65 million years ago. Marine reptiles went extinct then, too—all of them except for sea turtles, that is.

Seven types of sea turtles are still around today. The leatherback is the largest of them all. Leatherbacks can grow to more than seven feet (2 m) long. They can weigh more than 2,000 pounds (900 kg).

Other types of sea turtles have hard shells. Not leatherback sea turtles. They have thick, leathery skin. It's what gives them their name.

My assistant Mauricio (sounds like moh-REE-cee-oh) Handler was with me on the beach. As we watched, the giant female leatherbacks began to dig their nests and lay their eggs. Female leatherbacks always lay their eggs on warm, sandy beaches. Usually they return to the same beach where they were born.

Turtles in Trouble

Sadly, leatherback turtles are in danger of extinction. People have been hunting leatherbacks for centuries. But over the past 30 years, too many have been killed for their meat. People raided nests and took all the eggs. Today, new laws help protect nesting leatherbacks and their eggs. But they still face many dangers. They get tangled in fishnets. They get hooked on longlines meant to catch large fish. Houses and hotels have also been built on some of the leatherbacks' favorite nesting beaches.

I moved in close to one of the turtles. Leatherbacks only come out when it is dark. I knew the camera flashbulb would disturb her. So I would rely on the moonlight.

The turtle found a spot she liked. She made a shallow pit in the sand with her front flippers. Once she was comfy, she dug a deep hole with her hind flippers. She took long, deep breaths as she dug. To me, it was like a sound from the prehistoric (sounds like pre-hih-STORE-ick) past! She laid more than 80 round, white eggs in the hole. Then she covered them with sand.

We watched as the turtle headed back to the water. Having a chance to …

Want to know what happens next? Be sure to check out *The Whale Who Won Hearts!* Available wherever books and ebooks are sold.

INDEX

Boldface indicates illustrations.

MORE INFORMATION

To find more information about the animal species featured in this book, check out these books and websites:

Face to Face With Wild Horses, by Yva Momatiuk and John Eastcott, National Geographic, 2009

National Geographic Animal Encyclopedia, by Lucy Spelman, 2012

National Geographic Kids Everything Pets, by James Spears, 2013

Misty Meadows Farm
http://mistymeadowsfarmllc.com

The Grace Foundation
www.thegracefoundationofnorcal.org

San Diego Zoo
http://animals.sandiegozoo.org/animals/goat-sheep

Smithsonian National Zoo
http://nationalzoo.si.edu/Animals/KidsFarm/InTheBarn/Goats

**For Yael and Corbin,
two of the coolest young readers I know.
—A. B. B.**

CREDITS

Cover, Zuzule/Shutterstock; 4–6, courtesy of Sandy and Don Bonem;
12, © Taiga/Dreamstime; 16, 21, 26, courtesy of Sandy and Don Bonem; 30,
Makarova Viktoria/Shutterstock; 36–38, courtesy of the Grace Foundation;
43, branislavpudar/Shutterstock; 48, courtesy of the Grace Foundation; 54,
© Helmut Watson/Dreamstime; 58, courtesy of the Grace Foundation; 63,
© Duncan Noakes/Dreamstime; 68–70, courtesy of Molly Tillander; 77, ©
Jmaentz/Dreamstime; 80, courtesy of Molly Tillander; 85, FCG/Shutterstock;
90, courtesy of Molly Tillander; 94, © Scaliger/Dreamstime; 101, Brian
Skerry; 102, Brian Skerry; 108, Brian Skerry; 111, courtesy of Sandy and
Don Bonem

ACKNOWLEDGMENTS

Thank you to the following people who so graciously shared their
time and stories with me. This book would not have been possible
without them.

Sandy and Don Bonem, owners of the Misty Meadows Friesian herd

Beth DeCaprio and Lisa Dowling, friend and would-be friend of
Milkshake the cow

Susan, Tom, Molly, Jacob, and Alec Tillander, goat rescuers and
adopted family of Pony, Luna, and Thunder

Chad Artimovich, goat wrangler extraordinaire

I would also like to thank my editors, Marfé Ferguson Delano and
Becky Baines, along with the entire National Geographic Kids
Books staff who helped make this book possible.